best
easy
day hikes
Anza-Borrego

Bill Cunningham
Polly Burke

FALCON®
HELENA, MONTANA

AFALCONGUIDE®

Falcon® Publishing is continually expanding its list of recreational guidebooks. All books include detailed descriptions, accurate maps, and all information necessary for enjoyable trips. You can order extra copies of this book and get information and prices for other Falcon® books by writing Falcon, P.O. Box 1718, Helena, MT 59624 or calling toll free 1-800-582-2665. Also, please ask for a free copy of our current catalog. Visit our website at www.Falcon.com or contact us by e-mail at falcon@falcon.com.

© 2000 Falcon® Publishing, Inc., Helena, Montana.
Printed in Canada.

1 2 3 4 5 6 7 8 9 0 TP 04 03 02 01 00

Falcon and FalconGuide are registered trademarks of Falcon® Publishing, Inc.

Cover photo by Jeff Gnass.

Cataloging-in-Publication Data is on record at the Library of Congress.

CAUTION

Outdoor recreational activities are by their very nature potentially hazardous. All participants in such activities must assume responsibility for their own actions and safety. The information contained in this guidebook cannot replace sound judgment and good decision-making skills, which help reduce risk exposure, nor does the scope of this book allow for disclosure of all the potential hazards and risks involved in such activities.

Learn as much as possible about the outdoor recreational activities in which you participate, prepare for the unexpected, and be cautious. The reward will be a safer and more enjoyable experience.

CONTENTS

Map Legend

Interstate Highway/Freeway	00	City	⊞ or ◯
US Highway	00	Campground	▲
State, County, or Other Principal Road	00 000	Picnic Area	⊤
Forest Road	00	Building	■
Interstate Highway	═══⇒	Peak	⛰ 9,782 ft.
Paved Road	■═■═⇒	Elevation	9,782 ft. ✕
Gravel Road	═══⇒	River/Creek	∼
Unimproved Road	═════⇒	Spring	⌀
Trailhead	◯	Pass	)(
Parking Area	ⓟ	Mine Site	⚒
Main Trail/Route	∿	Sand Dunes	▨
Main Trail/Route on Road	∿	Overlook	◙
Alternate/Secondary Trail/Route	∿	Forest/Park Boundary	⌐ ⌐⌐
Alternate/Secondary Trail/Route on Road	∿	State/International Border	▬ ▪ ▬
One Way Road	One Way	Map Orientation	N ◆
Road Junction	☐	Scale	0 0.5 1 Miles

Overview Map of
Anza-Borrego Desert State Park

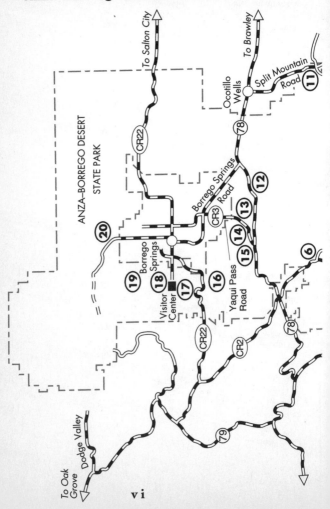

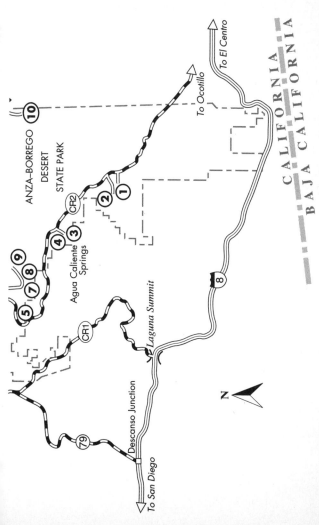

Ranking the Hikes

The following list ranks the hikes in this book from easiest to hardest. The ranking does not apply to hike options that may be listed for the hike.

Introduction

Best Easy Day Hikes Anza-Borrego is a condensed version of the Anza-Borrego Desert State Park section of *Hiking California's Desert Parks*. This compact guidebook highlights the easily accessible hikes that appeal to the broadest cross section of visitors. In particular, these hikes represent a superb sampler of the wonders of Anza-Borrego for those who only have a day or two to explore. This book is also handy for those desiring an easy start to a longer, more difficult outing.

At 600,000 acres, Anza-Borrego is the largest state park in the lower 48 states. Two-thirds of the park is protected as wilderness in 12 units. The park is named for Anza, the Spanish explorer who traversed the region in 1774, and Borrego, the Spanish name for bighorn sheep, in honor of those rare desert denizens that make these mountains and canyons home.

Elevations vary from 15 feet near Travertine Point in the northeast corner of the park to 6,193 feet atop Combs Peak on the west end. The park is a diverse geological wonderland of wide Sonoran Desert valleys, badlands, canyons, mountain ranges, year-round streams, and 25 oases with native California fan palms. Hikers can explore more than 110 miles of trails crisscrossing most sections of the park. Depending on weather, desert wildflowers erupt in spectacular spring bloom sometime between late February and early April.

In addition to desert bighorn sheep, nearly 60 mammal species, 270 kinds of birds, 27 snake species, and 31 lizard species live here, dispelling the myth that the desert is devoid of life. Many of these creatures are nocturnal and avoid humans. The botanical kingdom is equally diverse. An astounding 22 varieties of cacti grow in the park. Members of the ubiquitous cholla family of cacti range from the 3-inch fishhook cactus to barrel cactus that may exceed 8 feet in height.

With average daytime highs exceeding 100 degrees F during summer, it is advisable to hike in Anza-Borrego during the cooler seasons, when the temperature typically ranges between a comfortable 70 to 85 degrees F. Winter may bring rain showers. The heat of summer may bring occasional thunderstorms. Heavy rains in any season may produce flash flooding. Average annual rainfall at park headquarters is just under 7 inches.

Most of the hikes in *Best Easy Day Hikes Anza-Borrego* are less than 2 miles round trip and have less than 500 feet of elevation change. In general, they are well suited for families with small children. The trailheads for most of the hikes are accessible by paved highways, and of those that are not, only the Wilson Trail (Hike 16) requires a high-clearance vehicle.

We wish you happy trails on your "best easy" hikes through the richly varied Colorado Desert country of Anza-Borrego!

—*Bill Cunningham & Polly Burke*

How To Use This Guide

Types of Hikes
Loop: A loop hike starts and ends at the same trailhead without repeating all, or at least most, of the route. A portion of the hike may retrace a short stretch of the route. Round-trip mileage is indicated.

Out-and-back: Out-and-back hikes reach a specific destination and return on the same route. Round-trip mileage is indicated.

Shuttle: A shuttle hike begins and ends at different points and requires a car to shuttle between the two trailheads. The mileage given is the distance between the starting point and the ending point of the hike.

Use Trail: A use trail is an obvious footpath that is not maintained by the park or another agency.

Maps and Other Information
The map referred to as Earthwalk Press Anza-Borrego Region Recreation Map is a colorful 1:73,250-scale map of the Anza-Borrego area by Earthwalk Press. It is excellent for overall trip planning and navigating to the trailhead. Other useful maps include a set of eight 15-minute black-and-white topographic maps published by the Anza-Borrego Desert Natural History Association. In general, the more detailed 7.5-minute USGS quads for each hike are not needed, unless you plan to venture beyond the described route. Refer to the maps in this book, particularly for shorter hikes with signed trails.

The park charges a $5-per-vehicle day-use entrance fee. Dogs are $1 extra and cannot be taken on trails. Permits are not required for hiking, open desert camping, and backcountry travel.

The Anza-Borrego visitor center, located just west of Borrego Springs, is open daily from 9 A.M. to 5 P.M. from October through May. From June through September, it is open from 9 A.M. to 5 P.M only on weekends and holidays. A signed nature trail adjacent to the visitor center features a representative cross section of desert plants found in the Colorado (Sonoran) Desert.

For further information, contact: Anza-Borrego Desert State Park, 200 Palm Canyon Drive, Borrego Springs, CA 92004. The phone number for park headquarters is (760) 767-5311; you can get visitor center program information at (760) 767-4205, and camping reservations by calling 800-444-PARK. The spring wildflower hotline is (760) 767-4684. The park website is www.anzaborrego.statepark.org. This informative website, updated frequently, is a quick source for current park regulations, weather, and trail conditions.

How To Get There
The park is 80 miles east of San Diego at the eastern border of San Diego County. Interstate 8 passes the park's southern boundary on the way to El Centro. California 78 is the major access route to the central region of the park. Because this east-west highway evenly divides the park, the hikes presented in this book are listed as being either north or south of CA 78. San Diego County Road 22 is the highway to Borrego Springs, where the park visitor center is located.

Play It Safe

Wandering in the desert has a reputation of being a dangerous activity, thanks to both the Bible and Hollywood. Usually depicted as a wasteland, the desert evokes fear. With proper planning, however, desert hiking is not hazardous. In fact, it is fun, exciting, and quite safe.

An enjoyable desert outing, even a short one, requires preparation. You need to be equipped with adequate knowledge about your hiking area. In addition to this book and the maps suggested in the hike descriptions, carry a compass and know how to use it.

When traveling in the desert, on foot or by car, always carry water—and take the time to stop and drink it. Frequent water breaks are mandatory. It is best to return from your hike with empty water bottles. You can cut down on loss of bodily moisture by hiking with your mouth closed and breathing through your nose, and you can reduce thirst by avoiding sweets and alcohol.

Driving to and from the trailhead is statistically far more dangerous than hiking in the desert backcountry. But being far from the nearest 911 service requires knowledge about possible hazards and proper precautions to avoid them.

Dehydration
Plenty of water is necessary for desert hiking, even when walking a short nature trail. Carry one gallon of water per person per day in unbreakable plastic, screw-top containers, and pause often to drink. Carry water in your car as well so

you will have it when you return. As a general rule, plain water is a better thirst-quencher than any of the colored fluids on the market, which usually generate greater thirst. It is very important to maintain proper electrolyte balance by eating small quantities of nutritional foods throughout the day, even if you do not have an appetite.

Changeable Weather
The desert is well known for sudden weather changes. The temperature can change 50 degrees F in less than an hour. Prepare yourself with extra food and clothing, rain and wind gear, and a flashlight. When leaving on a trip let someone know your exact route, especially if you are traveling solo, as well as your estimated time of return. Do not forget to let them know when you get back.

Flash Floods
Desert washes and canyons can become traps for unwary visitors when rainstorms hit the desert. Keep a watchful eye on the sky. Never camp in flash-flood areas. Check on regional weather conditions at a ranger station before embarking on your backcountry expedition. A storm anywhere upstream in a drainage can cause a sudden torrent in a lower canyon. Do not cross a flooded wash. Both the depth and the current can be deceiving; wait for the flood to recede, which usually does not take long.

Lightning
Be aware of lightning, especially during summer storms. Stay off ridges and peaks. Also avoid shallow overhangs and gul-

lies because electrical current often moves at ground level near a lightning strike.

Hypothermia/Hyperthermia

Abrupt chilling is as much a danger in the desert as heat stroke. Storms and/or nightfall can cause desert temperatures to plunge. To avoid overheating or chilling, wear layers of clothes, adding or subtracting depending on conditions. At the other extreme, you need to protect yourself from sun and wind with proper clothing. The broad-brimmed hat is mandatory equipment for the desert traveler. Even in the cool days of winter—a delightful time in the desert—the sun's rays are intense.

Vegetation

You will learn quickly not to come in contact with certain desert vegetation. Catclaw, Spanish bayonet, and cacti are just a few of the botanical hazards that will get your attention if you become complacent. Carry tweezers to extract cactus spines. Wear long pants if traveling off trail or in a brushy area. Many folks carry a hair comb to assist in the removal of cholla balls.

Rattlesnakes, Scorpions, and Tarantulas

Desert "creepy crawlies" are easily terrified by unexpected human visitors, and they react predictably to being frightened. Do not sit or put your hands in dark places, especially during the warmer "snake-season" months. Carry and know how to use a snakebite kit. If bitten, seek medical assistance as quickly as possible.

Mountain Lions

The California desert is mountain lion country. Avoid hiking at night, when lions are often hunting. Instruct your children on appropriate behavior when confronted with a lion. Do not run. Keep children in sight while hiking; stay close to them in areas where lions might hide.

Unstable Rocky Slopes

Desert canyons and mountainsides often consist of crumbly or fragmented rock. Mountain sheep are better adapted to this terrain than we bipeds. Use caution when climbing; however, the downward journey is usually the more hazardous. Smooth rock faces such as in slickrock canyons are equally dangerous, especially when there is sand on the soles of your boots. On those rare occasions when they are wet, the rocks are slicker than ice.

Giardia

Any surface water, with the possible exception of springs flowing out of the ground, is apt to contain *Giardia lamblia*, a microorganism that causes severe diarrhea. Boil water for at least 5 minutes or use a filter system before drinking. Iodine drops are not effective in killing this pesky parasite.

Zero Impact

The desert environment is fragile; damage lasts for decades—even centuries. Courtesy requires us to leave no evidence that we were ever there. This ethic means no graffiti or defoliation at one end of the spectrum and no unnecessary footprints on delicate vegetation on the other. Following are the general guidelines for desert wilderness behavior.

Avoid making new trails. If hiking cross-country, a group should stay in one set of footprints. Try to make your route invisible.

Desert vegetation grows very slowly. Its destruction leads to wind and water erosion, and irreparable harm to the desert. Darker crusty soil that crumbles easily indicates cryptobiotic soils, which are a living blend of tightly bonded mosses, lichens, and bacteria. This dark crust prevents wind and water erosion and protects seeds that fall into the soil. Take special care to avoid stepping on this fragile layer.

Keep noise down. Desert wilderness means quiet and solitude, for both animals and humans.

Leave your pets at home. Dogs in particular are very disturbing to wildlife. Share other experiences with your best friend, not the desert.

Pack it in and pack it out. Desert winds spread debris, and desert air preserves it. Always carry a trash bag, both for your trash and for any you encounter. If you must smoke, pick up your butts and bag them. Bag and carry out toilet paper (it does not deteriorate in the desert) and feminine hygiene products.

Avoid water holes at night. Most desert animals are nocturnal, and most, like the bighorn sheep, are exceptionally wary of humans. Camping near their water source means they will go without water.

Camp in an already-used site if possible to reduce further environmental damage. If none is available, camp on ground that is bare. Leave your campsite as you found it. Better yet, improve it by picking up litter, cleaning out fire rings, or scattering ashes left by any inconsiderate predecessors.

Artifacts that are 50 years old or older are protected by federal law and must not be moved or removed.

Bury human waste 4 inches deep and at least 200 feet from water and trails. Do not burn toilet paper; many wildfires have been started this way. Bag it and carry it out.

Respect wildlife. Living in the desert is hard enough without being harassed by human intruders. Be respectful and use binoculars for long-distance viewing. Do not molest rare desert water sources by playing or bathing in them.

Enjoy the beauty and solitude of the desert, and leave it for others to enjoy.

1
MOUNTAIN PALM SPRINGS

Highlights: Six tightly clustered palm oases, where springs provide excellent birding.
Type of hike: Loop with out-and-back options.
Total distance: 5.1 miles.
Elevation gain: 320 feet.
Best months: October–April.
Maps: Earthwalk Press Anza-Borrego Region Recreation Map; USGS Sweeney Pass quad.
Parking and trailhead facilities: There is a signed trailhead and parking area at the end of the dirt road, with a campground nearby.

Finding the trailhead: From the Anza-Borrego park visitor center, go 1.9 miles east on Palm Canyon Road to Christmas Circle. From the circle, take Borrego Springs Road (San Diego County Road 3) south for 5.6 miles to the Y intersection, where you bear right (south). Continue on CR 3 (now Yaqui Pass Road) for 7.4 miles to the Tamarisk Grove intersection with California 78. Go right (west) on CA 78 for 7.4 miles to Scissors Crossing. Turn left (south) on San Diego County Road 2. Drive 31.8 miles south on CR 2. Shortly after mile marker 47, turn right (west) onto the dirt road for Mountain Palm Springs Campground. Continue 0.5 mile to the trailhead and parking area.

Mountain Palm Springs and Torote Canyon

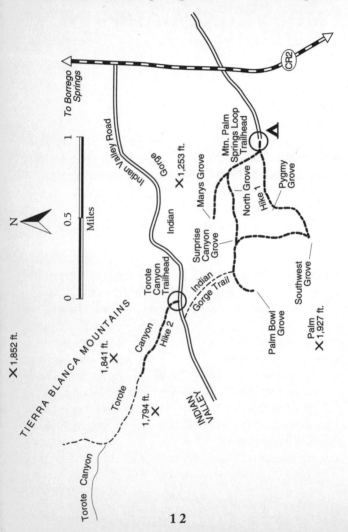

12

Key points:

0.0 From the trailhead, head west up the sandy wash.
0.8 Reach Pygmy Grove.
1.0 Turn left next to a single palm tree and head up the main wash.
1.2 The trail forks; stay right.
1.5 Reach Southwest Grove.
2.5 At Surprise Canyon, turn left (west).
3.0 Turn around at Palm Bowl Grove.
3.3 Indian Gorge Trail takes off to the left (north) side of Surprise Canyon.
3.5 Return to the Surprise Canyon Grove.
4.0 Pass North Grove.
4.3 Reach Marys Grove.
4.6 Hike back to North Grove.
5.1 Reach the trailhead.

The hike: This is a loop trail hike at the eastern edge of the Tierra Blanca Mountains, with several steep but short climbs and with two canyon branches to native palm groves.

The hike is best done as a complete loop to all six of the captivating palm groves in the Mountain Palm Springs complex. The two trails that lead from the trailhead head up sandy washes, one westward and the other to the north. It makes little difference which way you hike the loop, except that if you plan to take a side trip on the Indian Gorge Trail, it is preferable to begin on the south leg of the loop by heading west to the Pygmy Grove.

The native California fan palm is named for the shape of its leaves. As the tree produces new leaves at the top of its trunk, skirts of older leaves die and droop over the lower part of the tree, giving it the distinctive full look characteristic of the species. These groves are remnants of ancient savannahs. Here, water and shade attract scores of bird species, such as the hooded oriole, which weaves its nest on the underside of palm fronds. You also may spot a great horned owl, mourning dove, cactus wren, or western bluebird. In the fall, both birds and coyotes help regenerate the trees by eating their tiny fruits and leaving seed-laden droppings in new locations.

Beginning on the south end of the loop, head west up a sandy wash to the first small grove of four large palm trees at 0.4 mile. Continue up the main wash another 0.4 mile to the Pygmy Grove, named after the larger grove of short, fire-scarred trees. The third small grove consists of five trees in a tight cluster. From here, a rocky ravine leads to the right another 0.2 mile to a single palm tree. Turn left (southwest) up the main valley to a fork in the trail at 1.2 miles. Continue to the right another 0.3 mile to the sizable Southwest Grove. Pools of water and nearby elephant trees make this peaceful oasis an enjoyable interlude during the loop hike.

From the Southwest Grove, take a fairly distinct trail northward over a rocky ridge for 1 mile to Surprise Canyon. Turn left (west) and walk up Surprise Canyon another 0.5 mile to Palm Bowl, the largest and most luxuriant grove in the complex. The majestic palms are arranged like an orchestra in an amphitheater valley. Plan on allowing ample time to enjoy this magical place before hiking back down the wash.

Continue down the wash (the north leg of the loop), reaching North Grove at 4 miles. From here, Marys Grove is a 0.6-mile side trip to the left (northwest). From this junction the trailhead is only another 0.5 mile.

Options: If you plan to hike the complete loop, look for the signed Indian Gorge Cutoff Trail leading to the north on the way back down from Palm Bowl Grove. This old Indian trail is signed "0.5 mile to Indian Gorge." The actual distance is closer to 0.7 mile. The narrow, rocky trail gains 200 feet to the top of the ridge and then angles down to the left (northwest) into Indian Valley. The round-trip distance from Surprise Canyon to Indian Valley is 1.4 miles, providing yet more variety and a short extension to an already diverse hiking loop.

A shorter option from the trailhead is the 1.6-mile out-and-back hike to Marys Grove. The trail leads north from the parking area up a sandy wash, or, if you prefer firmer footing, up the right bank of the wash. You can catch a glimpse of palm trees 0.2 mile in the distance. The wash grows progressively rockier as you approach Marys Grove, where huge 30- to 40-foot palms tower above the rocky gorge. Of course, you can also visit Marys Grove as a 0.6-mile side trip on the Mountain Palm Springs Canyon loop hike.

2
TOROTE CANYON

see map page 12

Highlights: Elephant trees (*torote* in Spanish), and wide, remote basins ringed by rugged rock ridges.
Type of hike: Out-and-back.
Total distance: 1.2 miles.
Elevation gain: Minimal.
Best months: October–April.
Maps: Earthwalk Press Anza-Borrego Region Recreation Map; USGS Agua Caliente Spring, Arroyo Tapiado, Sombrero Peak, and Sweeney Pass quads.
Parking and trailhead facilities: Park alongside a dirt road with only a sign and monument to mark the spot.

Finding the trailhead: From the Anza-Borrego visitor center, drive east for 1.9 miles to Christmas Circle. Turn right on Borrego Springs Road (San Diego County Road 3) and drive south for 5.6 miles to the Y intersection. Turn right (south) on CR 3 (now Yaqui Pass Road) and drive 7.4 miles to the junction with California 78. Turn right (west) on CA 78 and drive another 7.4 miles to Scissors Crossing. Turn left (south) on San Diego County Road 2 and drive 29.6 miles to Indian Valley Road. Turn right (southwest) and drive 1.8 miles up the sandy road to the mouth of Torote Canyon, which is marked with a small sign. A monument entitled "El Torote" faces away from the road into the canyon.

Key points:
0.0 The trailhead is at the mouth of the canyon.
0.6 Arrive at a sizable "herd" of elephant trees.

Extended optional hike:
1.0 Reach the first wide basin.
1.5 At the canyon junction, the main Torote Canyon is to the left; turn right (north).
2.0 Arrive at a low pass above a second wide valley.

The hike: Hike up the sandy wash of Torote Canyon, which for the most part makes a good and easy-to-follow trail. You will need to scramble up and over an occasional boulder-clogged segment of the trail, but in general the going is easy enough to enjoy the canyon's remote surroundings. You will come to the first elephant tree on the left slope (south side) in less than 0.4 mile, but keep going for a good look at one of the densest "herds" of elephant trees in this bizarre tree's northernmost range at 0.6 mile.

The Spanish word *torote* means "twisted," referring to the gnarled growth pattern of the elephant trees, which are widespread in Mexico. At about 0.6 mile a large group of trees clings to the steep, rocky slopes above the canyon floor. Take time to get better acquainted with Borrego's rarest tree—feel its parchment-like bark, take note of its small, feathery leaves, and breathe deeply of its pleasant cedar-like aroma.

Options: To extend the out-and-back route to 4 miles, continue up the canyon. At about 1 mile, the canyon opens into the first wide valley, which stretches at least a half-mile to the northwest. At the head of the valley, the main Torote Canyon continues northwest up a boulder-strewn draw. Instead of hiking up the main canyon, follow what appears to be the main valley to the right (north). This leads to a short, tight canyon that opens after 0.2 mile to the second wide valley. Ascend the valley to a low pass at 2 miles. This is a good turnaround point for this pleasant journey. But head back only after you have given yourself enough time to savor the remote upper canyon's magic.

3
MOONLIGHT CANYON

Highlights: A colorful canyon, and interesting erosion patterns.
Type of hike: Loop.
Total distance: 1.5 miles.
Elevation gain: 350 feet.
Best months: October–April.
Maps: Earthwalk Press Anza-Borrego Region Recreation Map; USGS Agua Caliente Springs quad.
Parking and trailhead facilities: You will find a campground, hot springs, and a parking area at the end of the paved road.

Finding the trailhead: From the Anza-Borrego visitor center, drive east on Palm Canyon Drive for 1.9 miles to Christmas Circle. Turn right (south) at the circle on San Diego County Road 3 (also known as Borrego Springs Road) for 5.6 miles to the Y intersection. Bear right and continue south on CR 3 (now Yaqui Pass Road) for 7.4 miles to its intersection with California 78 just beyond the Tamarisk Grove Campground. Turn right (west) on CA 78 and go 7.4 miles to Scissors Crossing. At the crossing, turn left (south) on San Diego County Road 2 and drive 22.3 miles to the Agua Caliente Springs and campground turnoff. Turn right (south) and continue 0.5 mile to the trailhead at the parking area adjacent to the county park gate. There is a modest per per-

Moonlight Canyon
Squaw Peak and Squaw Pond

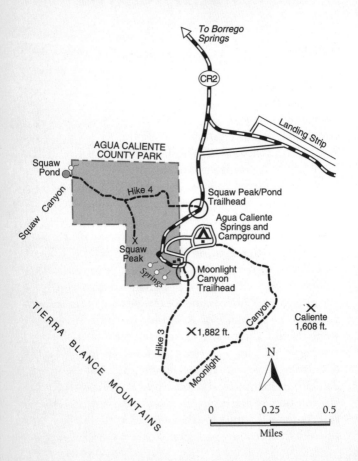

To Borrego Springs

CR2

Landing Strip

AGUA CALIENTE COUNTY PARK

Squaw Pond

Squaw Canyon

Hike 4

Squaw Peak/Pond Trailhead

Agua Caliente Springs and Campground

X Squaw Peak

Springs

Moonlight Canyon Trailhead

TIERRA BLANCE MOUNTAINS

Hike 3

X 1,882 ft.

Moonlight Canyon

X Caliente 1,608 ft.

N

0   0.25   0.5

Miles

son daily park entrance fee; the park is open from Labor Day to Memorial Day. The trailhead leaves from campsites 39 and 40, and returns near campsite 63.

Key points:
0.0 The trailhead leaves from campsites 39 and 40.
1.0 The trail enters the main wash.
1.1 Reach the trail junction.
1.3 Pass through the open ocotillo forest as the canyon broadens.
1.5 Return near campsite 63.

The hike: Although this trail lies outside of the Anza-Borrego park boundary, and there is an entry fee to the county park, it is definitely worth a visit. Interesting erosion formations, intermittent watery spots, and cozy side canyons combine to provide a series of discoveries as you follow the well-marked trail through the canyon.

The trail begins inauspiciously by climbing to a low ridge; it quickly drops to the stream bottom that goes up a rocky draw and into the canyon itself. Side washes and small canyons periodically invite further exploration as the main wash winds downward. Occasional steeply sloped spots require only simple scrambling on this otherwise easy hike. The rock formations, courtesy of centuries of water and earthquake activity, are endlessly fascinating. The variety of rock colors are also noteworthy. Sudden splashes of greenery where water exists—tamarisk and willow patches—punctuate the trip.

At 1 mile, the canyon empties into a wide, dry wash and

leads to a rock-lined trail at 1.1 miles that winds through an ocotillo forest at 1.3 miles. At 1.5 miles, you are back at the campground at site 63, down the hill from your starting point.

Option: The signed junction at 1.1 miles indicates a trail that leads to a short box canyon, which is well worth a side trip.

4
SQUAW PEAK AND SQUAW POND

see map page 20

Highlights: Scenic vista point; a lush desert spring oasis.
Type of hike: Out-and-back.
Total distance: 1.9 miles.
Elevation gain: 260 feet to Squaw Peak; minimal to Squaw Pond.
Best months: November–April.
Maps: Earthwalk Press Anza-Borrego Region Recreation Map; USGS Agua Caliente Springs quad.
Parking and trailhead facilities: There is a campground and hot springs near the trailhead, which is adjacent to a paved road.

Finding the trailhead: From the Anza-Borrego visitor center, head east on Palm Canyon Drive for 1.9 miles to Christmas Circle. Turn south at the circle on San Diego County Road 3 (Borrego Springs Road) and go 5.6 miles to the Y intersection. Bear right at the Y intersection and continue south on CR 3 (now Yaqui Pass Road) for 7.4 miles to its intersection with California 78, which is just beyond the Tamarisk Grove Campground. Turn right (west) on CA 78 and go 7.4 miles to Scissors Crossing. At the crossing, turn left (south) on San Diego County Road 2 and drive 22.3 miles to the turnoff for Agua Caliente Springs. Turn right (south) and drive 0.5 mile to the trailhead at the parking area adjacent to the park entrance. The park charges a modest per person daily entrance fee, and is open from Labor Day to Memorial Day. The trailhead is directly north of the ranger station. Cross the parking lot to a low ridge on the right next to the campfire circle, and take the path that leads to the campground amphitheater and Squaw Peak and Squaw Pond.

Key points:
0.0 Trailhead.
0.1 At the trail junction, turn left (south) to the Squaw Peak overlook. Take the trail to the right (northwest) to Squaw Pond.
0.3 Reach the Squaw Peak overlook.
0.6 Return to the trail junction.
0.7 Head up the Squaw Canyon wash.
1.2 Arrive at Squaw Pond.
1.9 Return to the trailhead.

The hike: From the Agua Caliente Springs parking area, pick up the trail to Squaw Peak and Squaw Pond near the campfire circle just above the ranger station and park entrance. Climb 0.1 mile to the ridgetop trail junction. Take the left (south) trail 0.25 mile to 1,450-foot Squaw Peak. From the junction, the trail switchbacks up 150 feet to an overlook of the Carrizo Valley and Badlands and the more distant Vallecito Mountains at 0.3 mile.

To reach Squaw Pond, drop back to the junction at 0.6 mile, and continue left (west) down to the sandy Squaw Canyon wash. Head up the well-traveled wash at 0.7 mile, passing clumps of honey mesquite, a food staple for early-day Cahuilla Indians. Cylindrical spikes of yellow flowers adorn the mesquite in late spring.

Squaw Pond is 0.5 mile up the wash at 1.2 miles. Coyote, bobcat, and a host of smaller animal tracks tell the tale of their visits to this desert spring oasis, which is shaded by dense willow and a single palm tree. Bring your binoculars for excellent birding at Squaw Pond. The surrounding hillsides are dotted with barrel and cholla cactus.

After savoring this tranquil setting, the most direct route back to the trailhead is to simply walk back down the wash, which intersects the road just below the parking area at 1.9 miles. In so doing, you will avoid the additional climb back over the ridge to the trail junction.

After the hike, you might enjoy a soak in Agua Caliente's mineral hot springs. A shallow outdoor pool averages around 95 degrees F and is open during the day. A larger indoor Jacuzzi pool is kept slightly warmer. The natural hot water source is an offshoot of the Elsinore Fault.

Box Canyon Overlook
Foot and Walker Pass

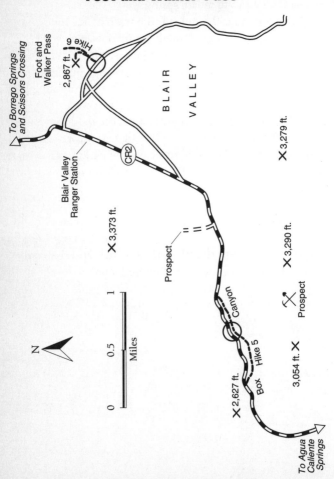

To Borrego Springs and Scissors Crossing

Foot and Walker Pass

Hike 6

X 2,867 ft.

BLAIR VALLEY

X 3,279 ft.

Blair Valley Ranger Station

CR2

X 3,373 ft.

Prospect

X 3,290 ft.

Prospect

Canyon

Box Hike 5

X 3,054 ft.

X 2,627 ft.

N

0   0.5   1

Miles

To Agua Caliente Springs

26

5
BOX CANYON OVERLOOK

Highlights: Historic Southern Emigrant Trail and Butterfield Overland Stage Route.
Type of hike: Out-and-back.
Total distance: 0.4 mile.
Elevation gain: Minimal.
Best months: October–April.
Maps: Earthwalk Press Anza-Borrego Region Recreation Map; USGS Earthquake Valley quad.
Parking and trailhead facilities: You will find a signed parking pullout with a historical marker adjacent to the paved highway at the trailhead.

Finding the trailhead: From the Anza-Borrego visitor center, go east 1.9 miles on Palm Canyon Drive to Christmas Circle in Borrego Springs. Turn south on San Diego County Road 3 and go 5.6 miles to the Y intersection. Bear right and continue south on CR 3 (now Yaqui Pass Road) for 7.4 miles to California 78. Turn right (west) on CA 78 and go another 7.4 miles to Scissors Crossing. Turn left (south) on San Diego County Road 2, and continue 9 miles. About 0.6 mile south of mile marker 25 on CR 2 is the Box Canyon parking pullout, which is on the south side of the road.

Key points:
0.0 The trailhead and overlook.
0.2 Reach the historic trail.

The hike: Much of Anza-Borrego's history coincides at this spot!
The Southern Emigrant Trail and the Butterfield Overland
Mail Route once traversed this arduous low mountain pass.
The historical marker is right by the highway; the overlook of
the trails is 250 feet farther east. From the overlook you can
spot two routes etched into the earth. The track left by the
Mormon Battalion, created in 1847, is the higher one; the
Butterfield Stage found an easier path in 1858.

Of greater historical significance is that General Kearny
and the "Army of the West," led by Kit Carson, passed
through Box Canyon a few days before the battle at San
Pasqual. This conflict was the deadliest battle of the Mexican War in California. General Kearny and his surviving
soldiers went on to fight in the battles at San Gabriel River
and La Mesa, thereby securing possession of California for
the United States. The trail was later called the Southern
Emigrant Trail because of the many prospectors and set-
tlers who traveled the route on their way west after 1847.

By following the path down to the trail itself at 0.2 mile,
you quickly get a feeling for the obstacle this rocky ridge
represented for travelers. The various historic travelers cut a
detour around the box canyon, but their efforts have eroded
with time. To follow a piece of the trail itself, take the slop-
ing trail down to the right to a wooden post. At this point,
the trail coincides with the wash. Occasional wooden posts
mark the historic wash trail.

Option: Follow the gently graded wash down for 0.7 mile to a pullout, where CR 2 almost touches the wash. The hike parallels the highway but is wholly hidden in the small canyon to provide a feeling of seclusion and communion with the hundreds of previous pioneer users of this trail segment.

Return to the overlook via the wash, not the highway. The narrow blind curves make the roadway dangerous at this point.

6
FOOT AND WALKER PASS

see map page 26

Highlights: Historic site of Butterfield Overland Stage Route.
Type of hike: Out-and-back.
Total distance: 0.2 mile.
Elevation gain: Minimal.
Best months: October–April.
Maps: Earthwalk Press Anza-Borrego Region Recreation Map; USGS Earthquake Valley quad.
Parking and trailhead facilities: There is a signed parking area with a historical monument at the trailhead.

Finding the trailhead: From the Anza-Borrego visitor center, go east 1.9 miles to Christmas Circle. Turn south on Borrego Springs Road (San Diego County Road 3) and go 5.6 miles to the Y intersection. Bear right (south) and continue on CR 3 (now Yaqui Pass Road) for 7.4 miles to the intersection with California 78. Turn right (west) on CA 78 and go another 7.4 miles to Scissors Crossing. Turn left (south) on San Diego County Road 2 and go 6.3 miles to Blair Valley turnoff, which is on your left (east). The Foot and Walker Trail Historical Monument is 0.3 mile from the turnoff on the north side of the valley.

Key points:
0.0 The trailhead and historic marker are on the hill.
0.1 Reach Foot and Walker Pass.

The hike: This short trail provides an excellent orientation to the Blair Valley region, with its layers of human use, from prehistoric (pictographs and morteros) to historic (pioneer routes through Box Canyon and Foot and Walker Pass) to recent (the Marshal South home on Ghost Mountain) times.

Here, where its route went past the entrance to the valley, the Butterfield Overland Stage had difficulty with the pass, especially if the coach had a heavy load. Often passengers had to hop out and walk—hence the name of the pass.

From the pullout on the dirt road below the hill, a use trail goes up the rise to a historic marker. A second use trail goes through the pass itself, where old wheel ruts are still visible. A brief hike to Foot and Walker Pass, at 0.1 mile, reminds us of the arduous conditions faced by nineteenth-century desert travelers.

Ghost Mountain, The Morteros, and Pictograph Trail

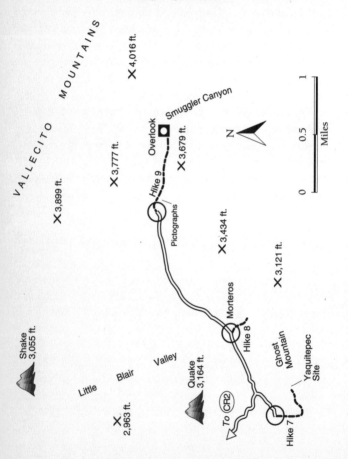

VALLECITO MOUNTAINS

Shake 3,055 ft.

X 3,899 ft.

X 2,963 ft.

X 3,777 ft.

X 4,016 ft.

Little Blair Valley

Quake 3,164 ft.

To CR2

Pictographs

Hike 9

Overlook

Smuggler Canyon

X 3,679 ft.

X 3,434 ft.

X 3,121 ft.

Morteros

Hike 8

Ghost Mountain

Yaquitepec Site

Hike 7

N

0   0.5   1

Miles

7
GHOST MOUNTAIN

Highlights: Historic, remote site of early home; spectacular views.
Type of hike: Out-and-back.
Total distance: 2 miles.
Elevation gain: 420 feet.
Best months: October–April.
Maps: Earthwalk Press Anza-Borrego Region Recreation Map; USGS Earthquake Valley quad.
Parking and trailhead facilities: There is a parking area at the end of a dirt road.

Finding the trailhead: From the Anza-Borrego visitor center, drive east for 1.9 miles to Christmas Circle in Borrego Springs. Turn south on San Diego County Road 3, then drive 5.6 miles to the Y intersection. Bear right at the Y intersection and continue south on CR 3 (now Yaqui Pass Road) for 7.4 miles to the intersection with California 78. Turn right (west) on CA 78, and go another 7.4 miles to the intersection with San Diego County Road 2 at Scissors Crossing. Turn left (south) on CR 2. Blair Valley is on your left (southeast) at mile 23, 6.3 miles southeast of Scissors Crossing. Turn left onto the dirt road. The Ghost Mountain parking area is 2.3 miles from CR 2.

Key points:
0.0 Trailhead.
1.0 Reach the Ghost Mountain summit (3,400 ft.) and Marshal South home.

The hike: Marshal South was a poet and an early refugee from civilization. He fled with his wife and three children in the 1930s to this remote desert mountaintop, named Yaquitepec. This hike is an interesting mixture of scenic splendor and devastating squalor. The landscape is breathtaking in its stark beauty, while the Souths' adobe cabin was primitive at best. The remains of the family's 15-year existence on top of a mountain peak in this valley creates a striking contrast with the awesome views in every direction. No water is available; the remains of a cistern system sit on the boulders near the cooking area. Fuel is also nonexistent. Living here must have been hard work, considering the lack of essential supplies.

From the parking area at the base of the mountain, the path snakes its way to the mountaintop with a series of steps and switchbacks. Marshal South may not have been terribly practical about location, but he did have some simple engineering skills. He built quite a trail, complete with steps carved into rocks on some of the steeper stretches. It is thought-provoking to imagine transporting food and water up this hillside and rearing three children in such a location.

When you arrive at the house site at 1 mile, the ruins reveal how basic life was for the South family. This was no castle. Of course, the dwelling has fallen into disrepair, with nothing left but crumbling walls and foundations, but the ruins provide evidence of the primitive quality of life for the Souths.

Because both sunrise and sunset are spectacular from Ghost Mountain, visiting campers have used the two or three sites available here, apparently with no trouble from the ghost. However, to protect the homesite, the park does not encourage camping here. The South family surely enjoyed the view.

Many interesting tales exist among local residents about the family and its escapades. According to one source, Marshal South eventually left his family and the mountain, going to live with a lady librarian in a nearby town. Tanya South and the children left too, and eventually changed their name to avoid continued publicity.

8
THE MORTEROS

see map page 32

Highlights: An easy path to the site of Indian grinding holes cut into granite boulders.

Type of hike: Out-and-back.

Total distance: 0.5 mile.

Elevation gain: Minimal.

Best months: October–April.

Maps: Earthwalk Press Anza-Borrego Region Recreation Map; USGS Whale Peak quad.

Parking and trailhead facilities: There is a parking area at the end of a dirt road.

Finding the trailhead: From the Anza-Borrego visitor center, drive east on Palm Canyon Drive for 1.9 miles to Christmas Circle. Turn south on San Diego County Road 3. At 5.6 miles, bear right (south) at the Y intersection and continue for 7.4 miles on CR 3 (Yaqui Pass Road) to its intersection with California 78. Turn right (west) on CA 78 and go 7.4 miles to Scissors Crossing. Turn left on San Diego County Road 2 and go south 6.3 miles. Turn left (southeast) at mile marker 23 onto the road to Blair Valley, and follow the dirt road for 3.5 miles to the Morteros pullout.

Key points:

0.0 Trailhead.

0.2 Approach the Morteros.

The hike: A broad, sandy trail leads southeast from the parking lot to the site of a prehistoric village set against the rock-strewn hillside. The slight elevation gain provides a sweeping view of Little Blair Valley stretching to the northwest. Huge obelisk-like boulders frame the large horizontal granite stones into which the morteros, or mortar stones, were worn by a thousand years of grinding by the Kumeyaay Indians. Fortunately, the site, at 0.25 mile, has been respected by visitors and remains in the same condition as when the Native Americans departed, giving it a hallowed feeling.

9
PICTOGRAPH TRAIL

see map page 32

Highlights: Ancient pictographs, a scenic overlook.
Type of hike: Out-and-back.
Total distance: 1.2 miles.
Elevation gain: Minimal.
Best months: October–April.
Maps: Earthwalk Press Anza-Borrego Region Recreation Map; USGS Whale Peak quad.
Parking and trailhead facilities: There is a signed trailhead and parking area at the end of the dirt road.

Finding the trailhead: From the Anza-Borrego visitor center, drive east on Palm Canyon Drive for 1.9 miles to Christmas Circle. Turn south on San Diego County Road 3. At 5.6 miles, bear right (south) at the Y intersection and continue for 7.4 miles on CR 3 (Yaqui Pass Road) to its intersection with California 78. Turn right (west) on CA 78 and go 7.4 miles to Scissors Crossing. Turn left on San Diego County Road 2 and go south 6.3 miles. Turn left (southeast) at mile marker 23 onto the road to Blair Valley. Follow the dirt road for 3.6 miles to the sign for the Pictograph Trail; take this rough but passable road for 1.5 miles to the parking area and trailhead.

Key points:
0.0 Trailhead.
0.5 Reach the pictographs.
1.1 Complete the optional hike to the overlook.

The hike: Blair Valley has attracted human visitors for centuries. High above the desert, its temperatures are more moderate than those of its surroundings. Early inhabitants evidently found it comfortable, as do present-day hikers and campers.

A wide, sandy trail leads east from the parking lot up a gradual slope to a saddle 160 feet higher than the parking area. The trail becomes rockier as it climbs through pinyon pine–juniper vegetation. Over the saddle, at 0.5 mile on the right (south), is a large boulder with mysterious pictographs (identified incorrectly as petroglyphs on the topographic map) left by prehistoric residents of this high valley. These striking artifacts of an ancient culture have been well preserved in their remote, wild location. Hikers can pause to contemplate the meaning of these signs, which still puzzle archeologists. Left by the ancient Dieguena Indian Tribe, the red and yellow pictographs painted on the rocks may have relayed messages to travelers, or have some religious significance. Prehistoric graffiti represents a large investment of time and labor, so it is not to be taken lightly.

Your view of Little Blair Valley on the hike back to the parking area shows the value of this location to early desert dwellers. Residents enjoyed excellent visibility from this slope at the end of the valley. There is a sacred feeling about being in an area that was inhabited so many centuries ago.

Option: For expansive views and a bit more of a leg stretcher, continue about 0.6 mile farther down the sandy wash path to a sharply defined notch in a rocky ridge. The notch, at 1.1 miles, offers an overlook of Vallecitos Valley and the Vallecitos Mountains. Whale Peak (5,349 feet) is prominent to the northeast. This is truly one of the grandest views in all of Anza-Borrego. There is an abrupt drop-off above Smuggler Canyon—a 150-foot dryfall at the overlook—so keep an eye on overly adventurous members of your hiking party.

10
WIND CAVES

Highlights: Geologic features, an archaeological site.
Type of hike: Loop.
Total distance: 1.5 miles.
Elevation gain: 620 feet.
Best months: October–March.
Maps: Earthwalk Press Anza-Borrego Region Recreation Map; USGS Carrizo Mountain NE quad.
Parking and trailhead facilities: The signed trail and parking area are adjacent to a dirt road.

Finding the trailhead: From the Anza-Borrego park visitor center, take Palm Canyon Drive for 1.9 miles east to Christmas Circle; at the circle turn south on Borrego Springs Road (San Diego County Road 3). At the Y intersection at 5.6 miles, continue straight (southeast) on Borrego Springs Road. Go 6.6 miles to the intersection with California 78. Turn left (east) on CA 78 and go 6.7 miles east to Ocotillo Wells. At the main intersection in town, turn right (south) onto Split Mountain Road. Drive south on Split Mountain Road, past the Elephant Trees Discovery Trail, to the right (west) turn onto Split Mountain Road, which heads up Fish Creek Wash, at 10.8 miles. Drive up the sandy wash for 5.1 miles to a very small Wind Caves sign indicating the trail on your left (east). The trailhead is just south of the narrows

Wind Caves and Elephant Trees Discovery Trail

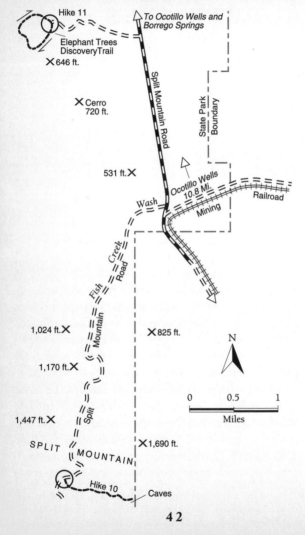

Hike 11

To Ocotillo Wells and Borrego Springs

Elephant Trees Discovery Trail

X 646 ft.

X Cerro 720 ft.

Split Mountain Road

State Park Boundary

531 ft. X

Ocotillo Wells 10.8 Mi.

Wash

Railroad

Mining

Fish Creek Road

Mountain

1,024 ft. X

X 825 ft.

1,170 ft. X

N

Split

0   0.5   1

Miles

1,447 ft. X

X 1,690 ft.

SPLIT MOUNTAIN

Hike 10   Caves

of the wash. The wash is not difficult for a passenger vehicle, but should definitely be avoided during wet or threatening weather. This road often requires a four-wheel-drive vehicle. Check conditions at the visitor center before taking this road.

Key points:
0.0 The trail climbs steeply from the wash to the plateau above.
0.3 Reach a variety of trails, all heading northeast. Take any one of the trails.
0.7 Reach Wind Caves.

The hike: The trip's excitement begins with the drive up the wash. Progressing upward from the valley floor, the wash approaches the rocky face of Split Mountain, then cuts through the mountain, with hardly any gain in elevation. The trailhead is beyond this narrow spot in the wash.

The first 0.2 mile of trail climbs from the floor of the wash to the ridge via a rocky but well-defined path. Behind you, the view of the Carrizo Badlands is spectacular. A variety of worn footpaths at 0.3 mile lead from the edge of the wash into the lands above; some of these routes are believed to be remnants of prehistoric use of the area. They all converge on the caves, so it does not matter which one you choose.

At a little over a half-mile up the trail, the caves come into view. The lower set of these fascinating sandstone formations has smaller alcoves; the caves on the higher level feature more spacious floor plans. There is an extraterrestrial quality about the site, due to both its ethereal appearance and the evidence that early Native Americans made use of these natural shelters. You will want to spend some time exploring the alcoves scattered around at 0.7 mile. The sand and wind-sculptured stoneworks resemble a piece of imaginative architecture or a deserted spaceship with rounded port holes.

On your return trip down Split Mountain Road, watch for additional wind cave formations high above the rim on the right (east). A visit to the caves makes you more observant when you scan the horizon in this rugged desert environment.

11
ELEPHANT TREES DISCOVERY TRAIL

see map page 42

Highlights: The diverse plant community of an alluvial fan and desert wash, including several rare and unusual elephant trees.
Type of hike: Loop.
Total distance: 1.5 miles.
Elevation gain: Minimal.
Best months: November–March.
Maps: Earthwalk Press Anza-Borrego Region Recreation Map; USGS Borrego Mountain SE quad.
Parking and trailhead facilities: There is a signed trail and parking area at the end of the dirt road.

Finding the trailhead: From the Anza-Borrego park visitor center, go east for 1.9 miles on Palm Canyon Drive to Christmas Circle. Take Borrego Springs Road south from the circle for 5.6 miles to the Y intersection. At the intersection, go straight (southeast) on Borrego Springs Road toward Ocotillo Wells. Borrego Springs Road meets California 78 at 6.6 miles. Go left (east) on CA 78 for 6.7 miles to Ocotillo Wells. Turn right (south) onto Split Mountain Road at the intersection in Ocotillo Wells and drive 5.9 miles to Elephant Trees Road. Turn right (west) and follow the dirt road for 1 mile to the parking area and trailhead.

Key points:
0.0 Trailhead.
1.5 Complete the loop.

The hike: This well-signed interpretive nature trail climbs gently up a rock-lined wash to a small "herd" of elephant trees. An informative brochure is available at the trailhead.

This most unusual elephant tree of the Sonoran Desert was not discovered and identified by botanists until 1937. This grove was long thought to be the northernmost group of elephant trees in California. However, in 1987 another grove of almost 200 elephant trees was discovered on the western slopes of the Santa Rosa Mountains, 21 miles farther north. Here, on the Elephant Trees Discovery Trail, there are only about 100 of these rare specimens. Although large elephant trees attain a height of only 10 feet, they tower above most other desert plants. They cling precariously to boulders and steep side slopes of the wash. Desert-dwelling Native Americans used the trees' red sap as medicine and to bring good fortune. Mayans and Aztecs burned the sap as incense and made a resinous dye for their clothing. Elephant trees are common to Baja California and the Mexican state of Sonora, but are found in only a few scattered canyons and washes of Anza-Borrego, the northernmost extent of their range.

This is an easy, educational loop winding up and down a rock-lined wash, with 17 plant identification stops keyed to the brochure. Most of the plants are common desert perennial shrubs such as burroweed, desert lavender, and brittlebush. Certainly, the most fascinating plants are the trail's namesake elephant trees, *Bursera microphylla*. The species name means "small-leaved," a common adaptation of desert plants to conserve water. The common name reflects the folded "skin" of the main trunk, much like that of an elephant.

This enjoyable 1.5-mile desert walk along a dry wash provides a fascinating glimpse of how vegetation copes with the harsh desert environment. For example, plants avoid dehydration by remaining short while shedding short, thick leaves.

Earth Narrows Trail

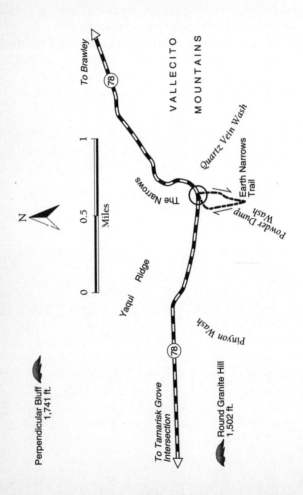

12
EARTH NARROWS TRAIL

Highlights: Chuparosa and pencil cholla, fault lines, interesting erosion patterns.
Type of hike: Loop.
Total distance: 0.5 mile.
Elevation gain: Minimal.
Best months: October–May.
Maps: Earthwalk Press Anza-Borrego Region Recreation Map; USGS Borrego Sink quad.
Parking and trailhead facilities: There is room to park alongside the paved highway at the unsigned trailhead.

Finding the trailhead: From the Anza-Borrego visitor center, go east on Palm Canyon Drive to Christmas Circle (1.9 miles); at the circle turn south onto Borrego Springs Road (San Diego County Road 3). Drive southeast for 5.6 miles to the Y intersection; continue on CR 3 (now Yaqui Pass Road) to the right (south). Go 7.4 miles to the intersection with California 78 just beyond the Tamarisk Grove Campground. Turn left (east) on CA 78 and continue 4.7 miles to the Earth Narrows parking area on the right (south). There is no sign. The parking area is a wide spot on the right (south) side of CA 78 immediately before the road takes a sharp right (north) turn through The Narrows.

Key points:
0.0 Trailhead.
0.5 Complete the loop.

The hike: The trailhead for this short nature trail is on a busy state highway, a major through route for trucks. It is immediately west of a narrow gap (labeled "The Narrows" on the topographic map) where Pinyon Ridge almost meets the Vallecito Mountains.

This signed, interpretive trail begins directly east of the parking area to your left. It is easy to miss stop #1, which is an important stop because the interpretive brochures are located there. The points along the trail focus on the geologic history of the region, revealed in the naked rock walls of this canyon. Fault lines, rock formation, and erosion are some of the lessons of the Earth Narrows Trail. The seven stops on the loop, which is 0.5-mile long, provide an introduction to the forces that created Anza-Borrego's landforms and topography.

The combination of igneous and sedimentary formations creates unusual geology. The igneous rock was formed deep within the earth and forced to the surface by huge tectonic forces; these granite masses are more than 100 million years old. Farther down the trail you will encounter rock that is 500 million years old. Originally mud and sand on the ocean floor, it has since been compressed and changed into metamorphic rock. At your feet, the desert's sedimentary layers attest to the wind's and rain's power to erode these ancient rocks to sand. The surface of the Earth Narrows canyon consists of an alluvial fan; heavy summer thunderstorms washed its sand and gravel down from the slopes above.

In addition to the various sediment deposits, the region is constantly affected by shifting tectonic plates. The Earth Narrows Trail is right on the intersection of the San Felipe Fault and the Yaqui Ridge Fault. The spider-webbed fault lines of southern California make the earth's surface quite dynamic, resulting in numerous earthquakes and tremors. Here in the desert, this geologic history is revealed on the barren walls of the Earth Narrows Trail.

Option: From the top of the loop, Powder Dump Wash continues another 0.2 mile to a sharp rise. For a longer hike, and to apply your newly acquired knowledge, you can continue up the wash before returning to the parking area.

Kenyon Overlook, Cactus Loop Trail, and Yaqui Well Nature Trail

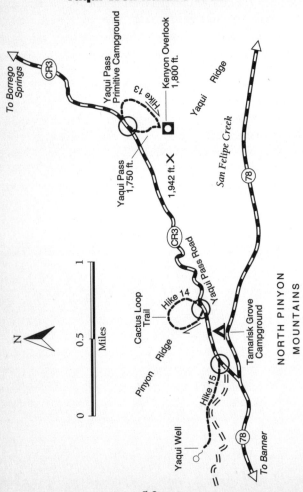

52

13
KENYON OVERLOOK

Highlights: Expansive views beyond the Vallecito Mountains as far as the Salton Sea.
Type of hike: Loop.
Total distance: 1 mile.
Elevation gain: Minimal.
Best months: October–April.
Maps: Earthwalk Press Anza-Borrego Region Recreation Map; USGS Borrego Sink quad.
Parking and trailhead facilities: At the trailhead, you will find a primitive campground, the signed trail, and a parking area just off the paved highway.

Finding the trailhead: From the Anza-Borrego visitor center, go east on Palm Canyon Drive for 1.9 miles to Christmas Circle. At the circle, take Borrego Springs Road (San Diego County Road 3) south for 5.6 miles to the Y intersection. At the Y intersection, turn right (south), staying on CR 3 (now Yaqui Pass Road). Drive 5.8 miles and turn left (east) into the Yaqui Pass Primitive Campground, where the northern trailhead is located.

After hiking the point-to-point loop trail to the Kenyon Overlook parking pullout, walk back down the highway about 0.2 mile to the starting point at the Yaqui Pass Primitive Campground parking lot.

Key points:
0.0 The trailhead is at the Yaqui Pass Primitive Campground and parking lot.
0.3 Reach the Kenyon Overlook.
1.0 Arrive at the Kenyon Overlook parking pullout on CR 3.

The hike: From the trailhead, take the signed trail uphill. The trail maintains a gentle up-and-down grade through a series of parallel gullies lined with yucca, creosote bush, silver cholla, ocotillo, beavertail cactus, barrel cactus, and brittlebush. The trail reaches its high point at a rocky ridge overlook at 0.3 mile. Turn left and walk about 30 yards to the overlook, which contains a monument in honor of William L. Kenyon, a noted desert conservationist and district park superintendent from 1947 to 1959.

From the overlook, the desert spreads out like the pages of a book. Beyond is a seemingly endless series of arroyos (washes) that deposit gravel and silt in delta-like fans, two or more of which are called bajadas. These bajadas support a dense mantle of agave, called mescal. On a clear day you can see the Salton Sea 30 miles to the east.

From the overlook return to the main trail, turn left (northwest), and drop gradually to the highway. At the highway make a right (northeast) turn and walk 0.2 mile to the Yaqui Pass Primitive Campground.

Option: To avoid walking the short distance on the highway, you may wish to hike back on the mile-long trail to the trailhead. In so doing, you will surely see interesting features and plants you missed on the way up. You can turn around at either the overlook or anywhere along the trail before it joins the highway.

14
CACTUS LOOP TRAIL

see map page 52

Highlights: A diverse array of cacti with late-season wildflowers due to the high elevation.
Type of hike: Loop.
Total distance: 1 mile.
Elevation gain: 230 feet.
Best months: October–May.
Maps: Earthwalk Press Anza-Borrego Region Recreation Map; USGS Borrego Sink quad.
Parking and trailhead facilities: You will find the signed trail and space to park across from the campground along the paved highway.

Finding the trailhead: From the Anza-Borrego park visitor center, take Palm Canyon Drive east to Christmas Circle. At the circle, take Borrego Springs Road (San Diego County Road 3) south for 5.6 miles to a Y intersection. Bear right (south) and continue on CR 3 (now Yaqui Pass Road) for 7 miles to Tamarisk Grove Campground, on your left (south). The signed Cactus Trail Loop trailhead is across from the campground entrance. Park in the shade of the tamarisk trees along the south side of the highway.

Key points:
0.0 Trailhead.
0.5 Reach the ridgetop.

The hike: This short, easy-to-follow trail begins as a sandy winding path and becomes rockier as it leads up the canyon. Signs identify jumping cholla, beavertail cactus, and salt-bush. When driving through the desert, the vegetation often looks monotonous and even dead. But when you stroll up the canyon on the Cactus Loop Trail, you notice the remarkable diversity of desert plant life as well as the variety of adaptive strategies necessary for desert survival. Perhaps most impressive are the teddy-bear cholla that attain a height of six feet.

The nature trail leads up the wash in a gentle ascent to the ridge's high point at 0.5 mile. Interpretive signs on the first part of the trail provide opportunities to stop and notice the vegetation that survives in this environment. On the ridge, too, you will have reason to pause and enjoy the magnificent view of the San Felipe wash and the vast mountain landscape.

From the ridge, the trail winds gently down the slope to the trailhead on CR 3. Overgrown brittlebush obscures the exit sign, but the trail itself is clear. You emerge just slightly east of your starting point, so it is only a short walk along the road back to your car.

15
YAQUI WELL NATURE TRAIL

see map page 52

Highlights: Diverse and abundant cacti, birding at the watering hole.
Type of hike: Out-and-back.
Total distance: 2 miles.
Elevation gain: Minimal.
Best months: October–April.
Maps: Earthwalk Press Anza-Borrego Region Recreation Map; USGS Tubb Canyon and Borrego Sink quads.
Parking and trailhead facilities: There is a trailhead sign and space for parking along the paved highway. The campground is nearby.

Finding the trailhead: From the Anza-Borrego park visitor center, go east for 1.9 miles to Christmas Circle. At the circle, turn south onto Borrego Springs Road (San Diego County Road 3). After 5.6 miles, bear right (south) onto Yaqui Pass Road (also CR 3). Continue for 7 miles to Tamarisk Grove Campground, which is across the road from Yaqui Well Nature Trail. Park along CR 3 outside the campground and cross the highway to the trailhead.

Key points:
0.0 Trailhead.
1.0 Reach Yaqui Well.

The hike: This is a well-signed, varied nature trail, slightly longer than most of the other trails in the park. The trail begins at the highway, but quickly angles up a rise on a gentle but rocky slope, where you become enveloped in the desert. The interpretive signs are frequent and clearly situated to label the correct plant. Jumping cholla are the most numerous plants, but ironwood and desert mistletoe also appear here.

Approaching the well from the east, the trail becomes sandy and level for the last 0.6 mile. The foliage at the well, at 1 mile, contrasts sharply with the surrounding desert plants. A dense thicket of mesquite crowds around the watery seep. Hardy old mesquite and ironwood trees surround the area. The well is a popular watering spot for local animals, especially birds. Although you can drive to the well via the Yaqui Well Campground Road, the walk through the desert makes you appreciate this water more. During the spring and fall migrations, bird watchers enjoy sitting quietly and unobtrusively near the well to see the visitors stopping for a beverage.

After your own respite at the well, the return journey to the trailhead will seem very dry. The trail parallels the San Felipe Creek Road, an undeveloped track, but the hiker is unaware of the seldom-used route. Instead, this short desert walk feels like a deep desert experience.

16
WILSON TRAIL

Highlights: A remote ridge dotted with pinyon pine; sweeping vistas of the central region of the park.
Type of hike: Out-and-back.
Total distance: 3 miles.
Elevation gain: Minimal.
Best months: October–April.
Maps: Earthwalk Press Anza-Borrego Region Recreation Map; USGS Tubb Canyon quad.
Parking and trailhead facilities: There is a signed trail with a small parking area adjacent to a dirt road.

Finding the trailhead: To reach the trailhead, which is off Old Culp Valley Road, go 15 miles east of Warner Springs on San Diego County Road 22 (Montezuma Valley Road); or 10.5 miles east from the intersection of CR 22 and San Diego County Road 2. Old Culp Valley Road is 8 miles southwest of the Anza-Borrego visitor center on CR 22 (Montezuma Valley Road).

Take the Old Culp Valley Road south. Four-wheel-drive vehicles are recommended on this steep, sandy road. At 0.4 mile, stay right at the road junction. Continue on the main road, ignoring turnouts. The Wilson Trailhead is another 2.7 miles up the road—a total of 3.1 miles from CR 22—and is marked by a small sign with a turnaround parking area just below a ridge dotted with sage, creosote, and granite boulders.

Wilson Trail

Montezuma Valley Road

To Visitor Center and Borrego Springs △

To Warner Springs ◁

CULP VALLEY

Old Culp Valley Road

CR22

✕ 3,182 ft.

Baker 4,084 ft.

✕ 4,146 ft.

N

0   0.5   1
Miles

Hike 16

PINYON

Overlook □
4,260 ft.
✕

Pinyon Spring (dry)

GRAPEVINE HILLS

Mount Wilson 4,573 ft.

RIDGE

Key points:
0.0 Trailhead.
1.5 Reach the ridgeline with scenic views and rock outcrop-
     pings.

Optional extended hike:
5.0 The old jeep trail disappears; the primitive trail contin-
     ues.
5.5 The use trail disappears; hike north to the overlook.

The hike: This long east-west trail follows the old Pinyon
Ridge jeep track, which is now closed to vehicular travel.
The trail and mountain are named for an early day Borrego
Valley cattle rancher.

The trail climbs moderately the first 0.6 mile to the ridgetop, with panoramic vistas of the Vallecito Mountains open-
ing to the southeast. It then gradually descends for 0.5 mile
to a broad saddle adorned with a heavy mantle of juniper,
cholla, and agave. After another 0.4 mile, the trail tops out
on a high ridge. An outcrop of sparkling, light-colored granite boulders lies just to the right (south) at 1.5 miles.

The remoteness of a high desert setting combined with
wide vistas make this a pleasant spot at which to linger. It is
also a good turnaround point for a representative sample of
the west-central region of the park, high in the Grapevine
Hills. The trail traverses a transitional mix of desert and
mountain flora, including yucca, cholla, manzanita, juniper,
and pinyon pine.

Option: The firm, sandy trail can be hiked for another 3.5 miles. For the first mile beyond the ridgetop overlook, the sandy track levels, climbs, and levels again. In a few places the trail is somewhat overgrown by vegetation, but all you have to do is look ahead 50 yards or so and you will easily spot the remnants of the two-track jeep trail.

At about mile 2 (from the trailhead), the trail climbs steeply for 0.2 mile, weaving between large boulders, then drops for 0.1 mile. This is followed by a steep 0.2-mile climb to a high side ridge. The route then drops slightly and levels out for another mile. The ridge is sprinkled with a few pinyon pines and cedar, which add variety to the mix of high desert flora.

The old jeep trail appears to end about 5 miles from the trailhead, after climbing gradually to a downed post with a cement base. A more primitive path marked by rock cairns leads steeply up through thick brush for about 0.2 mile. The path tops out in a saddle between the rocky points, including 4,573-foot Mount Wilson, and continues across a broad, open plateau for another 0.3 mile. Here, the sandy path disappears as the slope begins to drop eastward.

Before heading back to the trailhead, walk about 100 yards north to the rock-lined lip of the ridge for stunning views of Borrego Springs, the Salton Sea, and surrounding desert basins and ranges fading far into the distance. This remote stretch of the Grapevine Hills is used extensively by mountain lions, bobcats, and coyotes, as evidenced by abundant scat along the trail.

17
CULP VALLEY OVERLOOK

Highlights: Wide views of Borrego Valley, Coyote Mountain, and the Santa Rosa Mountains.
Type of hike: Out-and-back.
Total distance: 0.6 mile.
Elevation gain: Minimal.
Best months: October–May.
Maps: Earthwalk Press Anza-Borrego Region Recreation Map; USGS Tubb Canyon quad.
Parking and trailhead facilities: There is a signed trailhead and space for parking along the paved highway.

Finding the trailhead: From the Anza-Borrego visitor center, drive 0.5 mile east on Palm Canyon Drive and turn right (south) onto San Diego County Road 22 (Montezuma Valley Road). Continue for 9.5 miles; the twisting, curving road climbs above the valley floor into Culp Valley. Turn right (north) at the sign for Culp Valley Campground, which is a total of 10 miles from the visitor center. Take the right fork onto the road to the campground. The trail to the Culp Valley Overlook leaves from the northern edge of the campground area.

Culp Valley Overlook

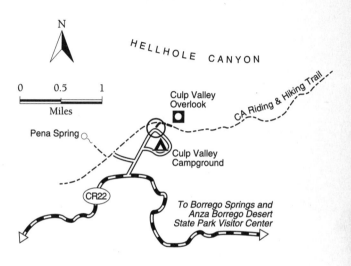

Key points:
0.0 The trailhead is at the Culp Valley Campground.
0.2 The trail intersects the California Riding and Hiking Trail; turn right (east).
0.3 Reach the lookout and turnaround point.

The hike: Culp Valley is a high valley (3,400 feet) on the southern edge of the San Ysidro Mountains. It was used for grazing cattle for many decades in the early half of the last century. Traces of its ranching past are noticeable, such as the stock watering facilities at Pena Spring (see option).

The trail to the Culp Valley Overlook is easily accessible from the main highway from Ranchita, so this hike gets lots of visitors. The view makes it a popular stop on most itineraries. The lookout point offers magnificent vistas of Hellhole Canyon and the desert expanse of the Borrego Valley and its surrounding mountains. This is not a hike for dashing out and then returning immediately to your car. When you reach the intersection with the California Riding and Hiking Trail at 0.2 mile, turn right (east) and explore a bit. There are several awe-inspiring overlooks, some even marked with "Photo Opportunity" signs. First-time visitors to the park might want to bring a park map to identify the sights at the overlook.

Several footpaths lead from the camping area to the overlook. The spray of paths should not be confusing as long as you keep your bearings and head south after enjoying the view. If you become so enchanted with the view that you continue to walk along the California Riding and Hiking Trail, you will find yourself descending steeply into the Borrego desert. It is 6 miles to the visitor center by this route. Carry several containers of water if you plan to do this longer hike.

Option: The hike to Pena Spring is an interesting short side trip. From the road that leads into the camping area, take the left fork to the road's end at 0.7 mile. The trail to the spring begins as an old jeep track but quickly becomes more primitive. Follow the trail for 0.3 mile to the artesian spring, an important source of water for wildlife in this high desert. Plan your visits to any water source during daylight hours because the wildlife needs access and privacy at night, when animals are most active. Restrain your pets in this area for the same reasons.

Panorama Overlook
Borrego Palm Canyon Nature Trail

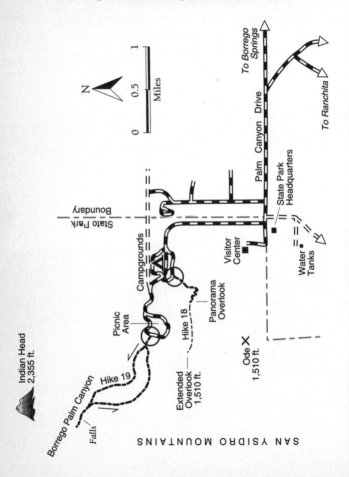

18
PANORAMA OVERLOOK

Highlights: The best all-around viewpoint of Borrego Springs Canyon and the adjacent valley.
Type of hike: Out-and-back.
Total distance: 1.4 miles.
Best months: October–April.
Elevation gain: 240 feet.
Maps: Earthwalk Press Anza-Borrego Region Recreation Map; USGS Borrego Palms Canyon quad.
Parking and trailhead facilities: There is a campground and signed trail off the paved road.

Finding the trailhead: From the Anza-Borrego visitor center at the intersection of San Diego County Road 22 and Palm Canyon Drive, follow signs north 0.8 mile to the Borrego Springs Campground. The trail starts near campsite 71. A level 1-mile trail from the visitor center northwest to the campground also intersects the Panorama Overlook Trail.

Key points:
0.0 Trailhead.
0.4 Reach the beginning of the switchback trail.
0.7 Arrive at Panorama Overlook.

The hike: From the signed trailhead next to the palm tree at campsite 71, the trail heads across a flat alluvial fan along the base of the rocky hillside for 0.4 mile to the "Overlook Trail" sign. Here, the trail begins to switchback up the slope. The clear but steep and rocky trail climbs 240 feet over a distance of 0.3 mile to an open knoll ringed by creosote bushes. The overlook offers a wide panorama from the eastern foot of San Ysidro Peak to Borrego Palm Canyon and Borrego Valley. Also in view are the Borrego Badlands, the Vallecito Mountains, and the Santa Rosa Range. With a good park map you will be able to identify many of the interesting features that surround you.

Option: For an even more expansive vista, continue west on a use trail, which is well-defined for the first 0.2 mile as it follows the initial level portion of the ridge. The use trail then winds upward through rocks and brush and sometimes all but disappears. Simply follow the main crest of the ridge leading toward the distant summit of San Ysidro Peak. At times the best footing is along either side of the actual ridgeline.

After another 0.4 mile and 300-foot gain, you will reach a somewhat level rocky ledge with several flat spots. These make for a wonderful overlook—a good place to sit and soak up the majestic desert scenery of canyons, alluvial fans, mountains, valleys, and jagged, exposed ridges. The palm groves of Borrego Palm Canyon are hidden from view, but take time here to scan the slopes for desert bighorn sheep. As with most mountainous use trails, this one is easier to find going down than up. This second overlook is a logical turnaround point for a vigorous half-day hike with spectacular desert scenery.

19
BORREGO PALM CANYON NATURE TRAIL

see map page 68

Highlights: A seasonal stream and waterfall at the upper end of California's third-largest palm oasis; a pupfish pool beside the trailhead parking lot. The sheep for whom the park is named are sometimes seen on canyon slopes above the oasis.

Type of hike: Loop.

Total distance: 3.5 miles.

Elevation gain: 500 feet.

Best months: October–April.

Maps: Earthwalk Press Anza-Borrego Region Recreation Map; USGS Borrego Palm Canyon quad.

Parking and trailhead facilities: The signed trailhead and picnic area are alongside the paved road.

Finding the trailhead: From the Anza-Borrego park visitor center, go north for 1 mile on the access road to Borrego Palm Canyon Campground and Picnic Area. There is a day-use fee for motor vehicles. The trail leaves from the northwest end of the picnic area.

Key points:
0.0 The trailhead is at the pupfish pond.
1.1 A sign on the south side of the footbridge indicates the loop trail for the return trip.

1.5 Arrive at the grotto and palm oasis.
1.7 Reach the overlook above the oasis.
2.4 Return to the footbridge; take the loop trail.
3.5 Arrive back at the trailhead.

The hike: This trail provides a spectacular introduction to the beauties of the desert. The interpretive brochure and the clear signs will help you become familiar with the plants and animals, geology, history, and ecology here. Ocotillo abound, as do honey mesquite, cheesebush, and chuparosa––the "hummingbird plant." Hummingbirds are plentiful, especially in spring. In winter and spring, water flows in the adjacent stream, with small waterfalls. Sharp-eyed hikers may spot reclusive bighorn sheep on the canyon's mountain slopes, especially in early morning or evening.

The trail begins at a pupfish pond, which holds the minnow-sized remnants of a prehistoric lake population. At 1.1 miles, you will pass the junction with the trail that you will take for the return leg of the hike.

At 1.3 miles, the walk up into the canyon changes radically. Before you is a dense palm grove in the narrow canyon. The trail winds through large boulders for 0.2 mile to a grotto adjacent to a small waterfall and one of the largest groves of California fan palms in the country. The grotto is a popular picnic and rest stop. Be careful not to encroach on the palm grove—the more than 50,000 visitors a year have caused some damage, especially to younger trees. Please remain behind the signed barricades, which are there to protect the fledgling palms.

For the more adventuresome hiker, a short steep climb via a trail above the oasis leads to an overlook 30 feet above the streambed at 1.7 miles.

Option: On the way back from the oasis, at 2.4 miles, an alternate route begins at the second footbridge you crossed on your way in. The trail goes along the higher canyon slope to the west, amid a slope of ocotillo. This route also leads back to the parking lot. It is slightly longer (0.5 mile more) and more difficult (100 feet of elevation gain) than the path along the stream, but you will enjoy a less-used trail with a loftier view of the canyon mouth below.

20
ALCOHOLIC PASS

Highlights: An historic trail with sweeping views of the northeastern corner of Anza-Borrego.
Type of hike: Out-and-back.
Total distance: 2.2 miles.
Elevation gain: 740 feet.
Best months: October–April.
Maps: Earthwalk Press Anza-Borrego Region Recreation Map; USGS Borrego Palm Canyon Clark Lake quads.
Parking and trailhead facilities: There is a signed trailhead with parking space adjacent to the dirt road.

Finding the trailhead: From the Anza-Borrego park visitor center, go east on Palm Canyon Drive for 1.9 miles to Christmas Circle. Continue 0.6 mile past the circle and turn left (north) on DiGiorgio Drive. At 5 miles the pavement ends. Continue north on Coyote Canyon Road, a rolling, soft dirt road, for 2.6 miles to the trailhead on your right.

Key points:
0.0 Head northeast from the trailhead.
1.0 The register is located west of the pass itself.
1.1 Reach Alcoholic Pass.

Alcoholic Pass

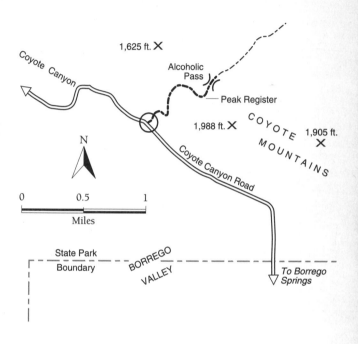

Coyote Canyon

1,625 ft. X

Alcoholic Pass

Peak Register

1,988 ft. X

COYOTE

1,905 ft. X

MOUNTAINS

N

Coyote Canyon Road

0   0.5   1

Miles

State Park Boundary

BORREGO

VALLEY

To Borrego Springs

The hike: For centuries, Alcoholic Pass has been used by the region's inhabitants to travel from Clark Valley (to the northeast) to Borrego Valley. The trail was created by countless moccasins before our hiking boots arrived. As you climb to the pass, with its sweeping view, you can imagine the variety of folks who have used the same pathway, as well as develop theories about the origin of the pass's curious name.

The first 0.2 mile of the hike heads up a sandy slope to a trail marker indicating a right turn up a side hill. Follow this ridge up a moderate incline. The trail becomes progressively rockier as it climbs to the trip register at 1 mile. At that point, you have reached a sandy plateau with sweeping views of the San Ysidro Mountains to the west and the Santa Rosa Mountains through the pass to the east.

The winding flat trail continues beyond the register. The summit of the pass is 0.1 mile farther upward. Here the trail is boulder-strewn, but the hardy hiker is rewarded with a great vista. At the summit of the pass, the valley on the other side begins as a wide sandy wash that slopes northeast to the plateau above Clark Valley. The mountains punctuate the skyline in the distance.

As you turn and retrace your steps to Coyote Canyon Road, you will enjoy views of the Borrego Valley and its mountainous rim.

Option: To extend the hike another 1 to 1.5 miles round-trip, continue down the other side of the pass along the open wash. About 0.6 mile beyond the pass, the wash fans to the northeast. This is a good spot to find a shady rock for lunch before heading back to the trailhead.

About the Authors

Polly Burke and Bill Cunningham are partners in the long trail of life. Polly, formerly a history teacher in St. Louis, Missouri, now makes her home with Bill in Choteau, Montana. She is pursuing multiple careers in freelance writing, leading group trips in the wilderness, and working with the developmentally disabled. Polly has hiked and backpacked extensively throughout many parts of the country.

Bill is a lifelong "wildernut," as a conservation activist, backpacking outfitter, and field studies teacher for The University of Montana. During the 1970s and 1980s he was a field representative for The Wilderness Society. He has written several books and dozens of magazine articles about wilderness areas based on extensive on-the-ground knowledge. He is the author of *Wild Montana*, the first in Falcon Publishing's series of guidebooks to wilderness and unprotected roadless areas.

Polly and Bill coauthored Falcon's *Hiking California's Desert Parks* (1996), *Wild Utah* (1998), and *Hiking the Gila Wilderness* (1999). Writing about the vast California desert has been especially rewarding because long ago the authors both lived close to the California desert—Bill in Bakersfield and Polly in San Diego. They have especially enjoyed renewing their ties to California while exploring the state's desert regions. They want others to have as much fun exploring it as they did.

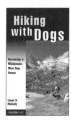

FALCONGUIDES ®Leading the Way™

All books in this popular series are regularly updated with accurate information on access, side trips, & safety.

HIKING GUIDES

Best Hikes Along the Continental Divide
Exploring Canyonlands & Arches
Exploring Hawaii's Parklands
Exploring Mount Helena
Exploring Southern California Beaches
Hiking Alaska
Hiking Arizona
Hiking Arizona's Cactus Country
Hiking the Beartooths
Hiking Big Bend National Park
Hiking the Bob Marshall Country
Hiking California
Hiking California's Desert Parks
Hiking Carlsbad Caverns & Guadalupe
  Mountains National Parks
Hiking Colorado
Hiking Colorado, Vol. II
Hiking Colorado's Summits
Hiking Colorado's Weminuche Wilderness
Hiking the Columbia River Gorge
Hiking Florida
Hiking Georgia
Hiking Glacier/Waterton Lakes
Hiking Grand Canyon National Park
Hiking Grand Staircase-Escalante
Hiking Grand Teton National Park
Hiking Great Basin
Hiking Hot Springs of the Pacific NW
Hiking Idaho
Hiking Indiana
Hiking Maine
Hiking Maryland and Delaware
Hiking Michigan
Hiking Minnesota
Hiking Montana
Hiking Mount Rainier National Park
Hiking Mount St. Helens
Hiking Nevada

Hiking New Hampshire
Hiking New Mexico
Hiking New York
Hiking North Carolina
Hiking North Cascades
Hiking Northern Arizona
Hiking Northern California
Hiking Olympic National Park
Hiking Oregon
Hiking Oregon's Central Cascades
Hiking Oregon's Eagle Cap Wilderness
Hiking Oregon's Mt. Hood/Badger Creek
Hiking Pennsylvania
Hiking Ruins Seldom Seen
Hiking Shenandoah National Park
Hiking the Sierra Nevada
Hiking South Carolina
Hiking South Dakota's Black Hills Cntry.
Hiking Southern New England
Hiking Tennessee
Hiking Texas
Hiking Utah
Hiking Utah's Summits
Hiking Vermont
Hiking Virginia
Hiking Washington
Hiking Wyoming
Hiking Wyoming's Cloud Peak Wilderness
Hiking Wyoming's Teton and Washakie
  Wilderness
Hiking Wyoming's Wind River Range
Hiking Yellowstone National Park
Hiking Yosemite National Park
Hiking Zion & Bryce Canyon
Wild Country Companion
Wild Montana
Wild Utah
Wild Virginia
Wilderness Directory

FALCON®

get
FALCON GUIDED

SCENIC DRIVING GUIDES

Scenic Driving Alaska and the Yukon
Scenic Driving Arizona
Scenic Driving the Beartooth Highway
Scenic Driving British Columbia
Scenic Driving California
Scenic Driving Colorado
Scenic Driving Florida
Scenic Driving Georgia
Scenic Driving Hawaii
Scenic Driving Idaho
Scenic Driving Kentucky
Scenic Driving Michigan
Scenic Driving Minnesota
Scenic Driving Montana
Scenic Driving New England
Scenic Driving New Mexico
Scenic Driving North Carolina
Scenic Driving Oregon

Scenic Driving the Ozarks including
    the Ouchita Mountains
Scenic Driving Pennsylvania
Scenic Driving Texas
Scenic Driving Utah
Scenic Driving Virginia
Scenic Driving Washington
Scenic Driving Wisconsin
Scenic Driving Wyoming
Scenic Driving Yellowstone and
    Grand Teton National Parks

National Forest Scenic Byways:
    East & South
National Forest Scenic Byways:
    Far West
National Forest Scenic Byways:
    Rocky Mountains

To order check with your local bookseller
or call Falcon at 1-800-582-2665.
www.Falcon.com

FALCON®

get
FALCONGUIDED

Field Guides

Bitterroot: Montana State Flower
Canyon Country Wildflowers
Central Rocky Mountain Wildflowers
Chihuahuan Desert Wildflowers
Great Lakes Berry Book
New England Berry Book
Ozark Wildflowers
Pacific Northwest Berry Book
Plants of Arizona
Rare Plants of Colorado
Rocky Mountain Berry Book
Scats & Tracks of the Pacific Coast
Scats & Tracks of the Rocky Mountains
Sierra Nevada Wildflowers
Southern Rocky Mountain Wildflowers
Tallgrass Prairie Wildflowers
Western Trees

FALCON®

FALCON GUIDES ®Leading the Way™

FalconGuides® are available for where-to-go hiking, mountain biking, rock climbing, walking, scenic driving, fishing, rockhounding, paddling, birding, wildlife viewing, and camping. We also have FalconGuides on essential outdoor skills and subjects and field identification. The following titles are currently available, but this list grows every year.

For a free catalog with a complete list of titles, call FALCON toll-free at 1-800-582-2665.

BEST EASY DAY HIKES SERIES

Anza-Borrego	Lake Tahoe
Beartooths	Mount Rainier
Boulder	Mount St. Helens
Canyonlands & Arches	North Cascades
Cape Cod	Northern Sierra
Colorado Springs	Olympics
Death Valley	Orange County
Denver	Phoenix
Glacier & Wateron Lakes	Salt Lake City
Grand Canyon	San Diego
Grand Staircase–Escalante and the Glen Canyon Region	Santa Fe
Grand Teton	Shenandoah
Joshua Tree	Yellowstone
	Yosemite

To order any of these books, check with your local bookseller or call FALCON® at 1-800-582-2665.
Visit us on the world wide web at:
www.Falcon.com

FALCON®

FALCONGUIDES ®Leading the Way™

Published in cooperation with Defenders of Wildlife, the Watchable Wildlife® Series is the official series of guidebooks for the National Watchable Wildlife Program. This highly successful program is a unique partnership of state and federal agencies and a private organization. Each full-color guidebook in the Watchable Wildlife® series features detailed site descriptions, side trips, viewing tips, and easy-to-follow maps.

WILDLIFE VIEWING GUIDES

To order any of these books, check with your
local bookseller or call Falcon® at
1-800-582-2665.
www.Falcon.com

FALCON®

get
FALCON GUIDED

BIRDING GUIDES

Birding Georgia
Birding Illinois
Birding Minnesota
Birding Montana
Birding Northern California
Birding Texas
Birding Utah

America's 100 Most
    Wanted Birds
Birder's Dictionary

FISHING GUIDES

Fishing Alaska
Fishing the Beartooths
Fishing Florida
Fishing Glacier National Park
Fishing Georgia
Fishing Maine
Fishing Montana
Fishing Wyoming
Fishing Yellowstone National
    Park

America's 100 Best Trout
    Streams
America's Best Bass Fishing

*To order check with your local bookseller
or call Falcon at 1-800-582-2665.
www.Falcon.com*

FALCON®

FALCONGUIDES ® Leading the Way™

www.Falcon.com

Since 1979, Falcon® has brought you the best in outdoor recreational guidebooks. Now you can access that same reliable and accurate information online.

❏ In-depth content, maps, and advice on a variety of outdoor activities, including hiking, climbing, biking, scenic driving, and wildlife viewing.

❏ A free monthly E-newsletter that delivers the latest news right to your inbox.

❏ Our popular games section where you can win prizes just by playing.

❏ An exciting and educational kids' section featuring online quizzes, coloring pages, and other activities.

❏ Outdoor forums where you can exchange ideas and tips with other outdoor enthusiasts.

❏ Also Falcon screensavers, online classified ads, and panoramic photos of spectacular destinations.

And much more!

Plan your next outdoor adventure at our website. Point your browser to www.Falcon.com and get FalconGuided!

FALCON®